China and Indian Ocean:

Strategic Interests and

Policies in the 21st Century

Khin Ma Ma Myo

Table of Contents

2

Introduction

"Whoever attains maritime supremacy in the Indian Ocean would be a prominent player on the international scene. Whoever controls the Indian Ocean dominates Asia"

Alfred Thayer Mahan

The Indian Ocean and the states on its littoral are of significant and growing importance. As Robert Kaplan, a US national security expert, argued, the Indian Ocean has become the center stage for the challenges of the 21st Century [1] with the growing maritime-strategic rivalry among India and China, the world's two most populous nations with a tetchy relationship.

The Indian Ocean is the third largest ocean in the world which is

---

1. Kaplan, R. (2009) Center Stage for the 21st Century: Power Plays in the Indian Ocean, *Foreign Affairs*, (March / April, 2009) http://www.realclearpolitics.com/articles/2009/03/rivalry_in_the_india n_ocean.html (accessed 2/11/2009)

3

about half of the size of the Pacific and slightly smaller than the Atlantic. Its northern part is surrounded by Africa, Asia and Australia to the extent that it tends to resemble a huge bay, which is highly contributed to its geopolitical and geostrategic significance. The most critical strategic and geopolitical factors in the Indian Ocean constitute the two large indentations in the southern coast of Asia around the Indian sub-continent - the Arabian Sea on India's west and the Bay of Bengal on the east.

By 1990, Britain had turned the Indian Ocean into a British Lake [2] and had military control over all the strategic important areas. At that time, only Ethiopia and Siam (Thailand) were remained as independent states, while all the other littoral states were in varying degrees of dependence on one of the European powers. In a post-war period, the United States appeared in the Indian Ocean with political, economic and military capacities and by the end of 1950s, it was the strongest power in the region along with the decline of the

---

2   Braun, D. (1983) *The Indian Ocean: Region of Conflict or 'Peace Zone'*, St. Martin's Press, New York, p.6

power of Britain.

Meanwhile, the Soviet Union started to show its interests in newly independent states with the appearance of Soviet fleet in the Indian Ocean by the end of 1960s. Thus, the Indian Ocean and its littoral states, have begun to show the characteristics of a major political region. The assertive global strategy of the two super-powers, referred to by the code names 'Diego Garcia' for the United States and 'Regular naval presence' for the Soviet contributed to this trend.

The other factor that characterized the region as an important strategic zone was the foreign policy of China which had been primarily based on power politics with the Soviet Union as its main opponent. China regularly labeled the extension of Soviet influence in the Indian Ocean region as the 'social imperialism[3] of the Soviet Union and establish instruments to gain political influence in the littoral states. For India, its options were clearly restricted within the

---

3   Peking Review, 27.6.1969

power struggles of the Soviet Union, the United States and China. During the 1970s, India's main goal appeared to keep all outside powers at such a distance from the territory to which it laid claim that they could no longer influence the balance of power in that area against India's interests.[4]

In fact, during the Cold War, the views on the global significance of the Indian Ocean differ on its strategic worth. To the Soviets, according to Davidov and Kremenyuk, 'the Indian Ocean and the countries round it are gradually becoming an independent geopolitical entity'[5] To the United States, according to Admiral Zumwalt, 'The Indian Ocean has become the area with the potential to produce majority shifts in the global power balance over the next decade '[6] and to Cohen, 'the Indian Ocean is an eventual third

---

4 Braun (1983), p. 131

5 Davidovv, . F. and Kremenyukv, . A. (1973) 'Strategiya SSHAV. Zone Indiyskovo Okeana', U.S.A.: Econ. Pol. Ideol. 5: 6-17 (Moscow)

6 Mugombaa., T. (1976) 'NATO, the Southern Oceans and SouthernA frica', A fr. Rev. 6: 15-33, p. 18

geostrategic region, with a globe-influencing character'.[7] Based on different views, the policies of the two superpowers and external powers of Britain, France, Japan, China and India had a mix of political, economic, social and strategic ingredients towards the Indian Ocean.

In the Post- Cold War Era, the balance of redistribution of power has more shifted to Asia. As Shambaugh argued, China's rise in world affairs is one of the main principal trends that define the new global order along with U.S. Military supremacy and unparalleled power, the EU's increasing coherence and economic weight, and the acceleration of technological and economic globalization.[8] China's increasing diplomatic, economic and military strength has compelled countries to rethink existing security strategies. In the Indian Ocean, there is a growing maritime- strategic rivalry between India and

---

7   Cohen, S. B. (1973) *Geography and politics in a world divided*, Oxford University Press, Oxford, p.63

8   Shambaugh, D. (2005) 'The New Strategic Triangle: U.S. And European Reactions to China's Rise, *The Washington Quarterly*, 28 (3), pp. 7 (7-25)

China. As their immediate security imperatives lie in the Indian Ocean, their strategic spheres have begun to overlap. China's defense assistance to Burmese military regime and exploration of access to the energy resources in Burma also intensify Sino-Indian rivalry.

For energy resources, approximately 60% of Beijing's oil crosses the India Ocean, specifically the Straight of Malacca, which is controlled by the US Navy. Thus, it is very obvious that the bulk of economic power of China lies in the hands of the sea lanes guaranteed by the US Navy. For Chinese strategic planners, there is a growing concern that the United States could cripple China by cutting off or blocking its energy supplies. Thus Beijing is continually looking for the ways on land across Central Asia and by the sea, which could circumvent the US-Controlled Strait of Malacca.[9] To gain its strategic ambitions in the Indian Ocean, China has tried to project the sphere of influence on the littoral states such as Sri Lanka, Burma, Pakistan,

---

9   Kaplan (2009)p. 23

etc. by developing closer relations.

It is therefore important to probe the deeper strategic interests and policies of China in the Indian Ocean region by addressing the questions like 'What are China's 21st century strategic interests in Indian Ocean?', 'How well is it managing relations with the major political actors in the region?', 'In what ways is China exploiting its relations with littoral states which have political and economic problems to its strategic advantage?' as well as to examine the future security environment by analyzing the controversial question of 'Will the future role of China in the Indian Ocean be stable and defensive or destructive and offensive?

China's Strategic Interests in the Indian Ocean

The Building of a strong and modern navy force must be necessary

to effectively fulfill its historic mission in the new stage of the new

century. China's territory boasts a large sea area and the navy is of

vital importance in defending state interests and safeguarding

national sovereignty and security

Hu Jintao, 10th CPC meeting

of the Navy, December 27, 2006[10]

---

10 Hu Jintao called for the building of a strong and modern navy
force while speaking at the tenth CPC meeting of the navy on
December 27, 2006, quoted in Matsuda, Y. & Saito, M. (2008)
'China: Hu Jintao Sets a Fres Course Amidst Diverse Challenges',
in Ogawa, S. (eds.) *East Asian Strategic Review: 2008,* The
National Institute for Defense Studies, Japan, The Japan Times,
p.101

China's Security Policy and Military Modernization Programs in the Post-Cold War Era

Since 1983, a concept of multipolarity *(duojihua)*[11] has occurred among Beijing's strategic scholars, while Beijing admitted a Washington-Moscow bipolar system. In a bipolar world, Beijing exploited super-power rivalry as a fulcrum to gain strategic leverage, economic and trade benefits, and global influence. After the United States extended diplomatic recognition to Beijing, Beijing leadership was looking forward to a strategic triangle in which China could act as a leader of the Third World by maneuvering between the United States and the soviet Union.

With the collapse of the old world order, Chinese political leaders began to feel vulnerable and marginalized in world affairs. Their view became clear and asserted that the world was evolving towards a multipolar system, as Qian Qiche stated in the 1991 year-end

---

11 Kim, S. (1991) 'Mainland China and a New World Order', in *Issues and Studie* 27, No.11 (November, 1991) p. 29

assessment of the international situations.[12] One of the Chinese

policy consultants, Xi Shuguang, presented the new multipolar

structure of the world with one system (the Western capitalist

system) and five 'geopolitical plates' such as European plate, African

plate, Middle East and Central Asia plate, Asia-Pacific plate and

North-South American plate).[13] With the perceptions of changes in

the international system, together with China's own immense

economic and political problems after the Tiananmen massacre,

Beijing leadership made a major foreign policy adjustment.

Suisheng Zhao identified three aspects of foreign policy adjustment

that are relevant to the multipolar international system.[14] First, Beijing

focused its policy objectives primarily on seeking better relations

---

12 Qiche, Q. (1992) 'Adhering to Independent Foreign Policy', in
   Beijing Review 34, N. 52, (Decmber, 1991- January, 1992), p.7-10
13 Shuguang, X. & Xinjiegou, S. (1992) *The New Structure of the
   World*, Chendu, Sichuan Renmin Chuban She
14 Zhao, S. (2004) 'Beijing's Perception of the International System
   and Foreign Policy Adjustment after the Tiananmen Incident', in
   Zhao, S. (ed.) *Chinese Foreign Policy: Pragmatism and Strategic
   Behaviour*, East Gate, New York

with, and greater influence on, neighboring Asia-Pacific countries by acting more as a regional power. Second, Beijing Policy towards the United States and other Western Powers became characterized by a combination of ever-ready concessions with an official anti-West sentiments. Third, Beijing struggled to establish an image as an independent and responsible member of the community of nations by taking more cooperative actions in multilateral initiatives and endorsed the call for the establishment of a 'new global partnership'.

However, by the end of twentieth century, Beijing leadership began to realize that the emerging security environment is not only characterized by the global shift to multipolarity, but also the rise of the U.S. Efforts to resist this transition and use its status as the sole remaining superpower. In 1997, one of the Chinese Scholars, made a comment on this issue as "The trend of global and regional multipolarization is more evident. However, the world is in a trial of strength over whether it will be multipolar or bipolar "[15]

---

15 Commentator, 'New Trends in the Current International Strategic Situation', *International Strategic Studies* (Beijing), No.1 (January,

Likewise, for Beijing's security consultants, the intent to delay China's emergence of great power in the Asia-Pacific region lies at the heart of U.S. Strategy and in their eyes, U.S superpower status depends on its diplomatic, economic and military ties throughout the Asia-Pacific region. Thus, Beijing security analysts crafted a carefully orchestrated campaign to determine the region's post-Cold War security architecture. Instead of seeking to replace the United States or eliminate its alliances, Beijing began to seek to form bilateral and multilateral cooperations and confidence-building measures for military alliances. Paul Godwin identified these efforts into three categories such as an intensified program of military diplomacy designed to ease regional concerns over China's defense policy, publications of Beijing's first defense white paper, and the presentation of a 'new model' of 'mutual understanding and co-operation' for regional security[16]

1997), p.1

16 Godwin, P. (1998) 'Force and Diplomacy: China Prepares for the Twenty-First Century', in Kim, S.(ed) *China and the World: Chinese Foreign Policy faces the new Millennium,* 4th edition, Westview Press, Oxford, p.182

Since then, China has been looking to cast itself in a positive light through all sorts of undertakings in military diplomacy. Beijing began to use 'military soft power' as the means of winning without war which means the capability to achieve militarily strategic goals through non-forceful methods and this power comes into play the realm of military democracy. Along with the Military Diplomacy, China enhanced its good-neighboring policy to share common security interests with the peripheral security environment. According to a Chinese security expert, Yan Xuetong, China's peripheral countries can be categorized into three in accordance with the degree of their agreement with China's terms of strategic balance. In his analysis, Yan stated that the countries which shared China's interest in developing a regional multipolarization in which China would be one of the most important strategic powers playing a balancing role would include Pakistan, North Korea, Burma, Nepal, Cambodia, Malaysia, Singapore, Russia and Central Asia states, the countries which hoped to maintain the current strategic balance in which the

15

United States had the strategically advanced position would include Australia, Canada, Indonesia, Thailand, the Philippines, Vietnam, New Zealand and India and the countries which had concerns over the rise of China and wanted to establish a multilateral mechanism in China's periphery to prevent China from becoming a security threat to their interests would include the United States and Japan.[17] To improve the relationships with these peripheral countries, Chinese leaders made a series of policy adjustments to establish a stable security environment.

With the success of Military Diplomacy and good-neighboring policy, China also sought to establish effective control over the Indian Ocean through military modernization campaigns. Among the PLA forces, Chinese Navy was being given priority in the allocation of resources and in the acquisition of military equipments. According to the Chinese naval strategy formulated by Central Military

---

17 Xuetong, Y. (1998) The rise of China: An Evaluation of the International Environment, *Tianjin Renmin Chuban She*, p. 234-236

Commission (CMC) Vice Chairman, Liu Huaqing, the navy's theater of operation would encompass mainly the first island chain, the outer littoral waters of that chain and the portions of the Yellow Sea, East China Sea, and South China Sea lying within the chain. He also asserted that the lines would gradually pushed out to the northern Pacific Ocean and the second island chain, in conjunction with the constant development economic strength and technology, and with further strengthening of the navy. He further stated that the protection of Chinese sea lanes (Figure- 1) must be one of the navy's strategic missions in wartime and necessary operating capabilities should include the ability to operate in waters adjacent to China's surrounding areas in the Indian Ocean.[18]

---

18 Admiral Liu was Vice Chairman of China's highest military body, the Central Military Commission, from 1989 until 1997. His naval strategic concepts were quoted in Li, N. (2009) 'The Evolution of China's Naval Strategy and Capabilities: From 'Near Coast' and 'Near Seas' to 'Far seas', *Asian Security,* 5 (2), (May 2009), p. 149 (144-169)

Moreover, Deputy Director of Political Department, Yao Wenhuai,[19] provided three recommendations for the outlines of naval strategy in 2007 as (1) more weight should be put on naval development since the traditional systems and structures of the army are no longer tune with today's realities, (2) since the navy has completed its transition to an offshore defense strategy, it should improve its general offshore operational capabilities within the first island chain perimeter while gradually enhancing blue-water maneuvering capabilities for a potential shift to blue-water defense; and (3) since the naval combat area is being enlarged from green water to blue water as a result of advances in the range and accuracy of modern weapons, the development of blue water maneuvering capabilities will become an increasingly critical and urgent task for national security.

According to East Asian Review (2008), the Chinese navy boosted its blue-water support capabilities through a resupply exercise that took place in the Indian Ocean in the early August, 2007 between the

---

19 Wenhuai, Y. (2007) 'Build a powerful Navy, Safeguard China's Maritime Strategic Interests', *Guofang 7*, p.6

18

supply ship *Weishanhu* and the guided missile destroyer *Guangzhou*.[20] Moreover, China has planned to deploy a fleet of nuclear-powered ballistic-missile submarines (SSBNs) and developed its Jin-class SSBN prototype with satellite pictures showing one such submarine berthed at the huge new Chinese naval base at Sanya, on the southern coast of Hainan Island in 2008.[21]

Furthermore, China's aircraft carrier development program has attracted global attention. In March, 2009, Chinese Defense Minister was quoted in the Oriental Morning Post newspaper by saying that "Among the big nations, only China does not have an aircraft carrier. China cannot be without an aircraft carrier forever," [22] According to the report by US Department of Defense in the early 2009, "Analysts in and out of government project that China will not have an

20 Matsuda, Y. & Saito, M. (2008)p. 103
21 Chellaney, B. (2008) 'Dragon in India's backyard', *Asia Age*, December 31, 2008
22 Oriental Morning Post, 24th March, 2009

operational, domestically-produced carrier and associated ships before 2015. However, changes in China's shipbuilding capability and degree of foreign assistance to the program could alter those projections. The PLA Navy is considering building multiple carriers by 2020."[23]

Taken together, the above doctrinal framework for high seas operations, along with the supply-capabilities and aircraft carrier development programs in the late 2010s, it is obvious that Chinese navy is designed to have a transition from offshore waters (Green Water) navy status to the high seas (Blue Water) navy status. Along with the modernization of the navy, China's maritime activities in the India Ocean clearly signals China's pursuit of sea power in the region.

---

23 Office of the Secretary of Defense (2009) *Military Power of the People's Republic of China 2009*, A report to the Congress, U.S. Department of Defense, http://www.defense.gov/pubs/pdfs/China_Military_Power_Report_2009.pdf (accessed on 12/12/2009)

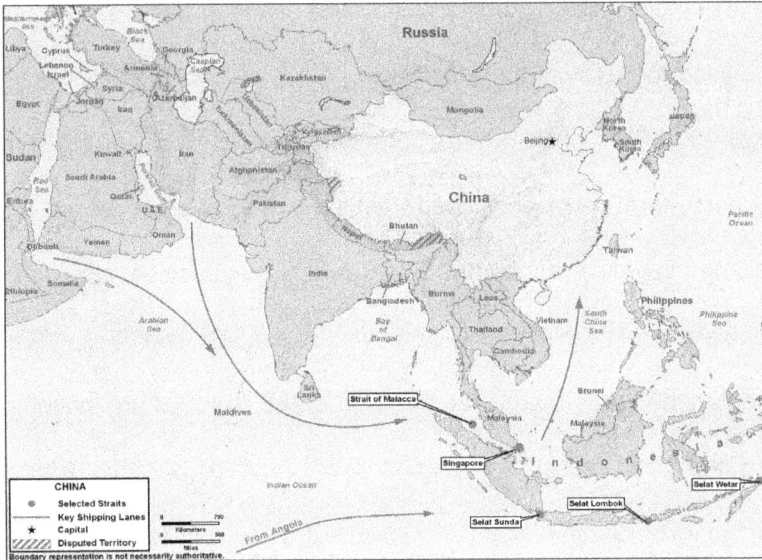

Figure 1. China's Critical Sea Lanes

China's Strategic Interests and Challenges in the Indian Ocean

For any nation, the rise and fall of the country depends on the strategic ability to use the land power, sea power and air power of national forces to achieve political and economic objectives. As sea power cannot be separated from its geo-political and geo-economic purposes, it has become pivotal in the history of economic development, military conflicts and rivalry among nations. Tangredi identified four factors that make sea power important such that (a) Over 70 percent of the world's surface is covered by ocean (b) Over 90 percent of international trade, which is measured in weight and volume, travels by water (c) The world's major cities and urban population lie within 200 kilometers of a coast line and (d)The international law provides for 'freedom of the seas' for any nation to use the open ocean for purposes of trade or defense without infringing on another country's sovereignty, subject to international agreements on pollution and exploitation of resources[24]

Thus, sea power has been marked as the determinant power for the fate of nations, especially in the era of emerging markets, trade and international co-operation and the sea lines of communications (SLOCs) is becoming the ultimate highways by which nations

---

24 Tangredi, S. (2002) 'Sea Power: Theory and Practice', in Baylis, J. al (eds) *Strategy in the contemporary world: An Introduction to Strategic Studies*, Oxford University Press, Oxford, p.115

communicate and interact in the new century. Like all other countries, China is now interdependent with a globalized market and involved with a growing number of international agenda such as global warming, energy security, nation-building, nuclear proliferation and global financial system.[25]

However, the geostrategic position of China is vulnerable along with the requirement of the heavy use of the Malacca Strait in south-east Asia, one of the significant strategic choke points which SLOCs travel through. The Malacca Strait (Figure-2) is a narrow and congested waterway separating Indonesia and Malaysia, with Singapore located at its southern tip and one of the world's most important waterways with the transit of more than 60,000 vessels each year. As Beijing continued to immerse itself into the international market, concerns about the safety and stability of its trade linkages and sea lanes have become one of the key strategic issues and Chinese leaders have come to view the Malacca Strait as

25 Shambaugh, p.7

a strategic vulnerability.

Figure-2: Strait of Malacca

About 50 per cent of ships passing through the Malacca Strait are sailing to and from one of the China's ports. Among them, the imports of raw materials, especially oil, which is vital for China's rapid economic development. Since 1993, China has had to import large volumes of crude oil and the demands for oil has been increasing

24

every year. As Chinese economy continued to depend on imported oil, especially from Middle East, any disruption to oil supply may have a serious impact on its economic survival. Thus, energy security has become a major concern for the Chinese leaders for several years and Malacca Strait has attracted the attention of Beijing leadership and security analysts.

In November 2003 President Hu Jintao[26] claimed that "certain major powers" were bent on controlling the strait, and called for the adoption of new strategies to mitigate the perceived strategic vulnerability. Later, by echoing the sayings of President, China Youth Daily expressed the 'Malacca Dilemma' as "It is no exaggeration to say that whoever controls the Strait of Malacca will also have a stranglehold on the energy route of China" [27] One Chinese scholar,

---

26 Speech by President Hu Jintao, cited in Storey, I. (2006) 'China's 'Malacca Dilemma', *China Brief,* 6 (8), James Stones Foundation, http://www.jamestown.org/programs/chinabrief/single/?tx_ttnews %5Btt_news%5D=31575&tx_ttnews%5BbackPid %5D=196&no_cache=1 (accessed on 13/12/2009)

27 China Youth Daily, June 15, 2004

Zhang Yuncheng, further suggested that whoever controls the Malacca Strait and the Indian Ocean could threaten China's energy security. [28] His remarks clearly reflects the fears of Beijing that ships carrying energy resources could be interdicted by the great powers' naval forces during a national security crisis.

Among Chinese security experts, fear of a worst case scenario of which would be a U.S blockade of China's oil imports from the Middle East has spread and triggered a rapid naval buildup by China. As You Ji argued, energy is crucially linked to national security for China and concerns over energy resources underlined the efforts of People Liberation Army (PLA) to back up a policy of cooperation with credible navy strength.[29] However, all China's maritime attempts to control events in the Indian Ocean would meet with Indian counter-

28 . Zhang Y., "The Malacca Strait and World Oil Security," *Huanqiu Shibao*, Dec. 2003, in. Guo Ling, "Experts Suggest Need to Build a 'Panamal Canal' in Asia," *Wen Wei Po*, Jan. 14, 2004.

29 Ji, Y. (2007) 'Dealing with the Malacca Dilemma: China's Effort to protect Energy's Supply', *Strategic Analysis,* 31(3), (May, 2007), p. 524 (523-542)

measures due to the Indian maritime strategy envisions.

Chinese scholar, Zhu Fenggang, identified the maritime objectives of New Delhi that may threaten energy security of China in the long-run. For Zhu, the objectives include (a) homeland defense, coastal defense, and control over maritime economic zones; (b) control of the waters adjacent to neighboring littoral states; (c) unfettered control of the seas stretching from the Strait of Hormuz to the Malacca Strait in peacetime, and the capacity to blockade these chokepoints effectively in wartime; and (d) the construction of a balanced oceangoing fleet able to project power into the Atlantic Ocean by way of the Cape of Good Hope and into the Pacific by way of the South China Sea.[30]

To reduce the strategic vulnerabilities that could be imposed by India and the United States, China, therefore, pursue a number of options to mitigate the dependency of oil and try to diversify its sources of

30 Fenggang, Z. (2006) "The Impact of the Maritime Strategies of Asia-Pacific Nations," Dangdai Yatai , 5, p. 34.

energy imports via new transit routes. Among them, the String of Pearls is one of the well-known emerging maritime strategy.

China's Emerging Maritime Strategy: The String of Pearls

The 'String of Pearls' strategy is designed to protect its energy security, negate the influences of U.S and India in the region and project power in the Indian Ocean. The strategy involves establishing a series of nodes of military and economic power throughout the region. Each node represents a pearl in the string and the string of these pearls extended from the coast of mainland China through the littorals of the South China Sea, the Strait of Malacca, across the Indian Ocean, and on to the littorals of the Arabian Sea and Persian Gulf. Some of the significant pearls include the upgraded military facilities on Hainan Island; the upgraded airstrip on Woody Island, located in the Paracel archipelago 300 nautical miles east of Vietnam; the construction of a container shipping facility in Chittagong, Bangladesh; the construction of a deep water port in Sittwe, Burma and the construction of a navy base in Gwadar, Pakistan, etc. (Figure-3)

28

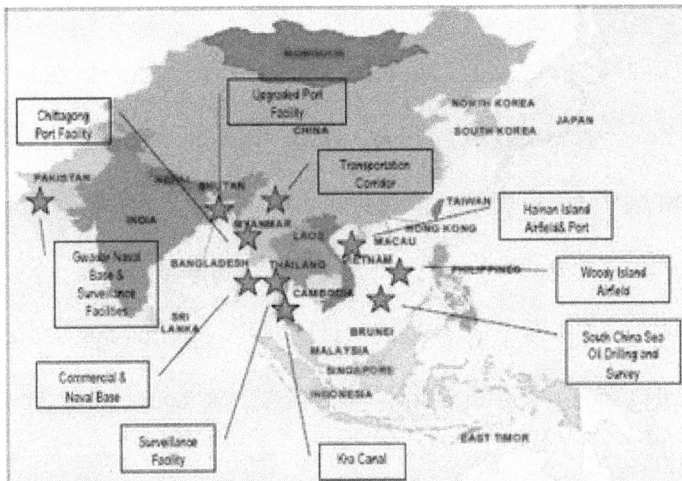

Figure 3- String of Pearls strategy

Christopher J. Pehrson described the emergence of the 'String of Pearls' as the manifestation of China's rising geopolitical influence through efforts to increase access to ports and airfields, develop special diplomatic relationships and modernize military forces that extend from the South China Sea through the Strait of Malacca, across the Indian Ocean, and on to the Arabian Gulf.[31] He identified

---

31 Pherson, C. (2006) *String of Pearls: Meeting the Challenges of China's Rising Power across the Asian Littoral*, Strategic Studies Institute, Carlisle, p. 3

29

three areas of China's strategic concerns such as regime survival, territorial integrity and domestic stability that are linked to the economic growth of China. He then concluded that as the strategic concerns depend on the security of SLOCs for energy and raw materials, energy security has become the principal motivation behind the 'String of Pearls'[32].This motive can be clearly seen in the following figure which shows both SLOCs and String of Peals. (Figure-4)

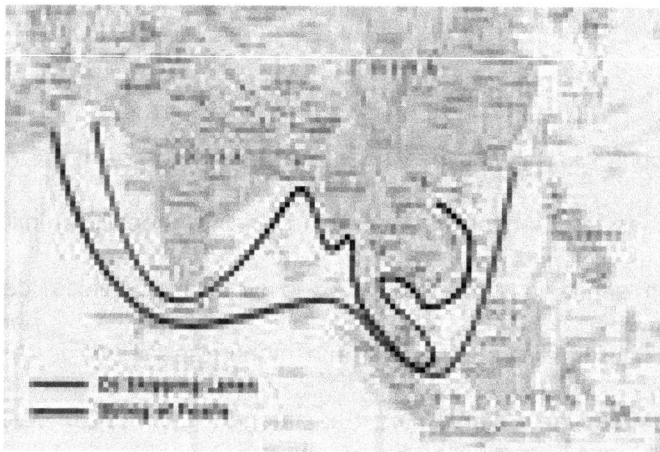

Figure 4- SLOCs and String of Pearls

32 Pherson, p.3

For India and the United States, the 'String of Pearls' mean the balance of power within the Indian and Arabian Gulf has now shifted away from the traditional Indian government management, backed up with U.S. military strength, but to China, backed up with regional diplomatic ties that dispense with the need to engage with either power as it provides a forward presence for China along the sea lines of communication that anchor China directly to the Middle East. In January 2006, India's Navy Chief, Adm. Sureesh Mehta, clearly mentioned about China's growing influence in the region by using the 'String of Pearls' strategy as "Each pearl in the string is a link in a chain of the Chinese maritime presence and could take control over the world energy jugular".[33]

Moreover, some analysts also argue that the ASEAN trading bloc, with China at its heart, and the massive emerging markets of India and the other Southeast Asian nations close by, will develop and

---

33 Speech by Indian Navy Chief, quoted in Bodeen, C. (2008) Indian Ocean is Chinese Lake: 'String of Pearls' threaten India, AP News, 29/8/2008

begin to rival that of the EU and the United States, and lessen China's dependence on these traditional export markets if the strategy continues without the development of regional conflicts.[34] However, some senior military officers from India have already presumed that there will be a regional conflict in the near future. One of the Indian Strategic Analyst, retired admiral Arun Prakash warned that "India has good cause to feel threatened because of China's quick expansion and opaque nature of their military plans. We must presume there will be a clash"[35] To the contrary, in April 2009, Hu Jintao assured that 'China would never seek hegemony, nor would it turn to arms races with other nations.'[36] while speaking before the delegations from the naval fleets of 14 nations at the Chinese port of Qingdao.

Nevertheless, China's 'String of Pearls' raised the international concerns over the power struggles in the Indian Ocean region and

34 Devonshire-Ellis, C. (2009) China's String of Pearls Strategy, China Briefing online, http://www.china-briefing.com/news/2009/03/18/china%E2%80%99s-string-of-pearls-strategy.html (accessed on 23/12/2009)
35 DNA Inida, May 11, 2009
36 China Youth Daily, April, 2009

some strategic analysts developed strategies and recommendations to counter China's String of Pearls. Major Lawrence Spinetta, from US Air Force developed a Land-based Air Power strategy[37] to control the littorals and cut the chains of the string. In contrast, Christopher Pherson provided several recommendations like protecting the commons against piracy and terrorism, hedging against the China's Threat and drawing China into the Community of Nations through engagement.[38]

The next section will explore China's strategic relationships with the major political actors in the Indian Ocean like the United States, Japan and India . How well China is managing relations with the current regional security guarantor in the Indian Ocean region, the United States; the local 'great power', India and the external economic power, Japan in the context of strategic interests?

37 Spinetta, L. (2006) 'THE MALACCA DILEMMA"- Countering China's String of Pearls with Land-based Air Power', Master's Thesis submitted to Air University, Alabama, p.48 (Unpublished)
38 Pherson, p. 22

China's strategic relations with India, Japan and the United States

"Good relations with the US is not only in the interests of the two peoples, but also beneficial to peace, stability and prosperity of the Asia-Pacific region, and the world at large"

Chinese President Hu Jintao[39]

US-China relationship

US-China relationship is one of the most important bilateral relations in the 21st Century. For several decades, it has been a product of fundamental changes in the international environment as well as the specified aspects of domestic political environment. For China, strategic relations with the United States makes the biggest policy challenge as there is no other country like the United States than can facilitate or hinder the achievement of Chinese goals and objectives

---

39 China Daily, 1st April, 2009

ranging from enhancing national security to expanding international recognition of China's rising power.

During the Cold War, US policy makers define the policy in terms of China as a friend in a larger conflict against the Soviet Union. On the other hand, Chinese leaders viewed the United States in the context of the international system defined by the competition of superpowers for global hegemony[40]. In the early 1970s, with the common interest in combating the 'Soviet threat', both Washington and Beijing ended the decades of Sino-American confrontation and strategic relations begun to expand leading to the establishment of diplomatic relations between China and the United States in 1979. Throughout the 1980s, diplomats from both sides engaged in a series of difficult negotiations to stabilize this so-called 'fragile relationship'.[41]

---

40 Levine, S. (1998)'Sini-American Relations' in Kim, S.(ed) China and the World: Chinese Foreign Policy faces the new Millennium, 4th edition, Westview Press, Oxford, p.182

41 Ross, R. (1995) 'Negotiationg Coperation: the United States and China (1969-89), Stanford University Press.

Despite of their efforts and attempts, US-China relationship was wracked by contention over issues such as human rights, international trade and territorial reunification during the 1990s. Two main things such as the collapse of the Soviet Union and the Tiananmen Square effectively encompassed in Sino-American relations in 1989. As Freeman stated as "And so the two things coming together meant that the previous policy of setting aside ideological differences in order to pursue practical cooperation between the United States and Chian effectively came to an end, symbolically, with the illfated December 1989 visit of National Security Adviser Brent Scowcroft to Beijing."[42], conflicts of interests, misunderstandings and suspensions made to accomplish common objectives.

To overcome these barriers of misunderstandings, Chinese President Jiang Zemin, urged to 'increase trust, reduce troubles,

---

42 Freeman Interview, quoted in Garrison, J. (2005) *Making China Policy: From Nixon to G.W. Bush*, Lynne Rienner, London, p. 124

strengthen cooperation and avoid confrontation ' [43] in 1992.

Thereafter, China adopted a multipronged approach to managing

strategic relationships with the United States. In bilateral terms,

Clinton's administration policy focused to engage China by

encouraging the forces of economic and political liberalization, while

Chinese leaders emphasized their desires for improved Sino-

American relations. Thus, in 1993, China and the United States

resumed their security dialogue, which Washington had suspended

in 1989 to protest Tiananmen affairs.

In 1997, China and the United States declared to build a constructive

strategic partnership in the twenty-first century, meaning that 'China

is not a potential adversary of the United States, much less an

enemy of the United States, instead it is a trustworthy partner for

cooperation'[44] By using this concept of 'strategic partnership',

Chinese leaders appeal to their major counterparts to identify

_____

43 People's daily, December 1, 1992

44 Chinese Premier Zhu Rongji defined the concept of strategic
   partner in his speech., People's daily, April 16, 1999

common interests and abandon the Cold War mentality. Joseph Cheng and Zhang Wankun identified the motivations of Chinese leaders behind this concept in accordance with China's strategic objectives, as "China wanted to secure a peaceful, stable international environment to pursue its modernization, promote global multipolarization and seek due recognition of China's status as an important pole in a multipolar world.[45] Obviously, there is no doubt that Chinese leadership had been engaging in developing a new strategic thinking and ideological positions in support of China's emergence as a major power in the 21st century since the end of the last century. To encounter a theory of 'China threat' with the rise of the power, Chinese leaders tried to forge a pattern of relations with the major powers, especially with the United States, which is based on equality, mutual respect, mutual checks and balances and cooperation.

---

45 Cheng, J. & Wankun (2004) 'Patterns and Dynamics of China's International Strategic Behaviour', in Zhao, S. (ed.) *Chinese Foreign Policy: Pragmatism and Strategic Behaviour*, East Gate, New York,p. 197

Regarding China's Strategic partnership, U.S President, Clinton, later argued that after his meeting with Jiang Zemin, he went to bed by thinking that 'China would be forced by the imperatives of modern society to become more open, and that in the new century it was more likely that our nations would be more partners than adversaries'.[46] In contrast to Bill Clinton, Bush administration in the early 21st century viewed China as a hostile rising power. In stead of using a strategic partner, Bush adopted the language of 'strategic competitor' and initial East Asian policy of Bush administration emphasized to consolidate relations with key allies like Japan in the face of threats posed by China.

However, U.S Secretary of State, Colin Powell, recognized the role of common interests by stating that 'Strategic partner China is not, but neither is China our inevitable and implacable foe. China is a competitor, a potential regional rival, but it is also a trading partner willing to cooperate in areas where our strategic interests overlap.

46 Clinton, W. (2004) *My Life*, Knopf, p.768

China is all of these things, but China is not an enemy, an our challenge is to keep it that way'[47] Later, immediately aftermath of the EP-3 crisis, which led to an Sino-American confrontation, high-level contacts between the United States and China resumed with a tangible working relationship to avoid similar confrontations.

In the context of Asia-Pacific region, the United States attempted to augment its political, economic and military relationships with China under the banner of 'transformational diplomacy' since 2006. It encouraged China to play a constructive role in the region, especially in the Six-party talks on the North Korean Nuclear issue with the expectation that China's involvement may provide the mechanism for peace and stability in North-East Asia. However, the US administration, policy think-tanks and strategic analysts were alarmed over several moves by China such as the rise of defense spending, modernization of the navy and maritime activities, the emergence of the 'String of Pearls' in the Indian Ocean and the

_____

47 Powell, C., Hearing before the Senate Foreign Relations Committee, January 21, 2007, quoted in Garrison, p. 170

deployment of Jin-class nuclear submarines.

For the United States, its strategic aims in the Indian Ocean are inextricably linked to the vast stretch of water, the emergence of terrorism and piracy, the vast energy resources and the movement of these energy resources to several economies via SLOCs. Its strategic interest might be primarily motivated by a desire to protect global energy markets. As over half of the world's oil supplies travel through sea lanes in the Indian Ocean, disruption of energy supplies would have a serious impact on the United States regardless of whether U.S. Supplies travel through these sea lanes or not.

The other motive relates to the control over the strategic choke points for energy security of China to deter the reunification efforts through the Use of Force. US has a long history of Support for Taiwan's security and in favor of protecting the island against forced surrender to the mainland rather than abandoning it.[48] Moreover, the

---

48 Romberg, A. (2009) "U.S. Strategic Interests in Northeast Asia: 2009 and Beyond",

41

refusal of protection would undermine the credibility of U.S Diplomacy in the region and the U.S treaty commitments to allies such as Japan and Korea. Thus the control over the strategic choke points in the Indian Ocean represent one of the major strategic advantages for the United States.

For several decades, the United States is the powerful security guarantor in the region to provide a public good by guaranteeing freedom of navigation throughout Asia's major SLOCs with the ability to project power with the blue water navy status. Thus the question of whether China could be identified as its potential major competitor in the Indian Ocean or not, might also depend on the U.S. Strategic policies towards China. As Pherson stated, 'If Washington assumes China is striving for regional hegemony and responds with an aggressive military posture, it could cause China to respond in kind, fostering a vicious cycle of military buildup and counterbalancing measures. A confrontation could become a self-fulfilling prophecy if

http://www.stimson.org/eastasia/pdf/USInterests2009.pdf
(accessed on 26/12/2009)

the United States fails to gauge China's intent accurately and inadvertently sends the wrong diplomatic, economic, or military signals"[49], U.S. Security strategy would have a major influence on China's future directions.

Sino-Japanese relations

China's relationship with Japan is very complex. In the 1950s, China viewed Japan as a contemptible U.S. Lackey and Beijing's relations with Japan ranged from hostility to chilly. However, in the wake of the Sino-Soviet splits in the 1960s, China began to seek trade partners and establish commercial links with Japan. Soon after the U.S. President's visit to China in 1972, Japan moved swiftly to establish diplomatic relations with China. By the beginning in 1982, China became the top recipient of Japanese official development assistance (ODA). Sino-Japanese relations are regularly reinforced by visits between the cabinet-ministers.

---

49 Pherson, p. 22

Despite of these economic linkages and high-level political leaders' contacts, there have some troublesome military and strategic issues since the end of the Cold War. As Donal Klein argues, China tended to see itself as a three-way informal alliance with Japan and the United States a mean of countering the Soviet Union during the Cold War.[50] However, China had expressed a lot of concerns over the rise of Japanese military power and Japan's security treaty with the United States. In the eyes of Chinese strategic analysts, the U.S.-Japan security treaty would 'check Japan's presumed ambitions to become a regional hegemon and to curb any Japanese military buildup' in terms of the best scenario, however, it may be 'the prospect of American and Japanese forces cooperating under the umbrella of the U.S.-Japan alliance in response to the use of force by China'[51] in terms of the worst scenario.

---

50 Klien, D. (1998) 'Japan and Europe in Chinese Foreign Relations', in Kim, S.(ed) *China and the World: Chinese Foreign Policy faces the new Millennium*, 4th edition, Westview Press, Oxford, p.142

51 Garrett, B. & Glaser, B. (1997) 'Chinese Apprehensions about Revitalization of the U.S.-Japan alliance', *Asian Survey*, 37 (4), p. 385-386

In the eyes of Japanese strategic analysts, Chinese actions like 'the unilateral claim to sovereignty regarding the Senkaku/Diaoyutai Islands; active role in the global arms trade, 'gunboat diplomacy' in the South China Sea and suspicious behavior on a host of arms control and disarmament issues [52] are of deep concerns for the Japanese security. With deep concerns, Japan has also taken a more critical position on China's efforts of military modernization. Thus, Japan has made China the major target of its national defense strategy. Due to these frictional forces in Sino-Japanese relations, Robert Sutter argued that Asia's future would hang on this antagonistic relationship as it could force other Asian Governments to choose sides that could split the region in ways not seen since the Sino-Soviet rivalry of the Cold War.[53]

Moreover, Japan sees Indian Ocean as an important strategic area that could make vulnerable to its emerging economic power,

---

52 Yomiuri Shimbun, March 17, 1997

53 Sutter,R. (2002) 'China and Japan: Troubled ahead?', The Washington Quarterly, 25 (4), (Autumn 2002), p. 39 (p.37-49)

therefore, the rise of China power in the region is perceived as a complex security challenge. Like China, Japan's economy heavily depends on the sea lanes and strategic choke point, the Malacca Strait. Thus, for the safe passage of ships through the Malacca Strait, Japan has long cooperated with Singapore, Malaysia and Indonesia in the areas of seabed mapping and navigation safety. While attempting cooperation efforts with these three countries, Japan focused on the cooperative capacity building among the other littoral states in the Indian Ocean.

With China's string of pearls strategy gaining ground as its fleet expands in the Indian Ocean, Japan made responses by modernizing its own naval fleets, enhancing US-Japan alliances and strengthening the strategic partnership with India. In May, 2007, Japan and the United States issued a joint statement calling for China to 'maintain consistency between its stated policies and actions' despite of the phrase used for China as a 'responsible international stakeholder'.[54] In terms of naval modernization, Japan

54 SCC Joint Statement(May 1, 2007) Alliance Transformation:

involved in the testing and development of the US Aegis fleet defense system in 2009[55]. As the system is designed to redress the potential threat from China, Japan's involvement could enhance the capabilities of the Japanese Maritime Self-Defense Force (JMSDF).

The Unite States and Japan have also sought to establish Asian-Pacific trilateralism by pursuing trilateral security dialogue with Australia and strengthening the strategic relationships with India as a strategic partner sharing common values. The emergence of a dialogue of democracies between U.S., Australia, Japan and India also forge Indo-Japanese alliance. From Chinese perspectives, these trilateral security cooperations could be perceived as the attempts to encircle or contain China as well. However, China's economic interests are well served by being able to cooperate effectively with Japan on trade, investment, energy efficiency,

---

Advancing United States-Japan Security and Defense Cooperation, http://www.mod.go.jp/e/d_policy/dp16.html (accessed on 1/1/2010)

55 'Rapid Naval Growth in Asia', *Defense Review Asia Magazine*, December, 2009

environmental protection, fisheries, and other issues of mutual importance. Thus, to avoid further military conflicts, China actively engaged in 'military diplomacy' with Japan since 2007. In November 2007, a Chinese missile destroyer visited the port of Tokyo, becoming the first Chinese warship to make a port call to Japan and in return, a Japanese Maritime Self-Defense Force (JMSDF) destroyer paid a call to the Chinese southern port of Zhanjiang in June 2008[56] Thus military and strategic affairs would depend on the warming up of the diplomatic relations and the main anchor of the strategic relations, i.e. economic ties between the two countries in the near future.

Sino-Indian Relations

During the 1950s, China and India made friends by working together in the promotion of the national independent movement in the Third World. However, they became enemies and encountered military clash in 1962. The root of the Sino-Indian war in 1962 was Tibet

---

56 ''Warship Visit Brings Message of Peace', China Daily, July 2, 2008

controversy. Misunderstandings between the two nations led to diplomatic clashes over Tibet, with Indian President Nehru's move to accommodate Tibet Leader, Dalai Lama. Tensions steadily increased between the two nations and Chinese forces entered part of Indian's administrative regions in 1961. Indian reacted with the Forward Policy stated as 'If the Chinese will not vacate the areas occupied by her, Indian will certainly drive out the Chinese forces.'[57] In response, Beijing leaders adopted the policy of 'armed co-existence' and launched simultaneous offensives on 20th October, 1962, later the war was ended with the declaration of cease-fire and withdrawl from the border disputed areas by Chinese forces. However, the military actions of China has been viewed by the United States as part of the policy of making the use of force to settle border issues and distract from internal issues[58] and has been still perceived by India as a humiliating defeat.[59]

---

57 Noorani, A. (1970) 'India's Forward Policy', The China Quarterly,No.43 (July-September 1970), p. 136 (136-141)

58 Lamb, A. (1964) The China-India Border: The origins of the Disputed Boundaries, London, Oxford University Press

59 Han, H. (1998) 'Sino-Indian relations and nuclear arms control', in

In 1964, China became a nuclear weapon state and there has been a sense of Chinese nuclear threat to India and the West since then. 10 years later, India's first detonation of a nuclear device occurred despite of the arguments for a non-nuclear weapon policy. With a nuclear race, Sino-Indian relations continued to deteriorate throughout the 1970s and 1980s. In the late 1980s, the relations began to improve with the high-levels ministerial visits and negotiations to settle border disputes. In 1988, both sides agree to establish a joint working group to settle a 'fair and reasonable settlement' and with the recommendations made by the joint working group, China and India signed two agreements on the 'Maintenance of Peace and Tranquility' and 'Confidence Building Measures' in 1993 and 1996, respectively.

Despite of the cultivation of friendly relations, Sino-Indian

---

Arett, E. (ed.) *Nuclear Weapons and arms control in South Asia after the test ban*, SIPRI Research Report No.14, New York, Oxford University Press, p.35

relationships has never stopped in three areas such as the Pakistan issue, Tibet issue and two segments of disputed border in the southern Himalayan Mountains and the Aksai Chin Plateau. In the eyes of the Indian strategic analysts, China was perceived as a threat to India. General Krishnaswami Sundarji, former chief of staff of the Indian army, wrote in 1995 that 'India needed both a nuclear and a conventional minimum capability to deter China and Pakistan,' and "if the Chinese use only tactical nuclear weapons, India would do likewise."[60] In the wake of the nuclear tests in India in 1998, Indian Minister of Defense, George Fermandes, publicly referred to China as 'India's enemy number one.'[61] Chinese leaders were furious by these comments and accused India of 'running against the international trend of peace.'[62]

However, the tests had not undermined China's engagement policy

60 Sundarji, K. (1995) 'Weapons of Mass Destruction: New Perspectives on Counterproliferation, Institute for National Strategic Studies, p. 55
61 Quoted in China News Digest-Global, December 12, 1998
62 China Daily, May 19, 1998, p. 4

towards India due to the successful bilateral trade relations. In 1999, Indian Foreign Minister visited China and Sino-Indian Security dialogue was established in 2000. Upon entering the 21st century, both leaders seek the common grounds for co-operation. In 2003, Chinese and Indian leaders signed the Joint Declaration on the Principles of Relations and Comprehensive Co-operation and clearly pointed out that the two countries would respect mutual concerns and should not have the threat of the Use of Force towards each other. In 2005, China-India joint communique was signed by the political leadership with the establishment of peace and prosperity-oriented strategic co-operative partnership.

Despite of these mature Sino-Indian relations, strategic analysts from both countries, nevertheless, perceive each other as potential adversaries and dangerous strategic rivals in Asia with global power ambitions. Indian strategic scholar, Mohan Malik, argues that Sino-Indian relations today constitute a new cold war and this cold war may well be the dominant feature of Asian geopolitics in the 21st

century.[63] Accordingly, a commentary in China Daily, stated that "The fact is that Japan, Australia, and India are respectively located at China's northeast, southeast, and southwest, and all are Asian powers, while U.S. power in the Pacific is still unchallengeable. Hence, should the"alliance of values" concentrating military and ideological flavors in one body take shape, it will have a very great impact on China's security environment."[64]

With respect to the Indian Ocean region, John Garver also points out the existence of security dilemma by focusing on Chinese ties to the littoral states in the Indian Ocean region more than India. In his analysis of the rise of China in the Indian Ocean region and India's counter-measures, he clearly stated the relationship as 'The metaphor of two scorpions in a bottle once used to describe USA-USSR relations during the mutual nuclear terror of the Cold War

63 Malik, M. (1999) "India-China relations in the 21st Century: The Continuing Rivalry", Brahma Chellaney edited, *Securing India's Future in the New Millennium*, Orient Longman, p.337-338
64 China Daily, 12 June, 2005

seems applied to the Sino-Indian relationship today.' by adding that 'The state of play in the Sino-Indian relationship is that Beijing is mobilizing pressure to compel New Delhi to acquiesce to an open-ended expansion of China's military links and security role in the Indian Ocean region and New Delhi is mobilizing counter-pressure on China via the Look East policy to compel Beijing to suspend, or, roll back, its deep and growing military involvement in the region.'[65]

For India, the north-east Indian Ocean is the area which is important for the supreme national security interest of 'Survival'. Like China, India's economic power depends on oil imports from the Gulf, which supplies 65% of its needs and perhaps more than 75% by 2015. At present, India has a stake in protecting maritime security and freedom of navigation along the ocean SLOCs to provide a growing economy. Moreover, the Indian Ocean affords directly access to the Indian landmass and represent the most vital challenge to Indian security emerging from the maritime basin. Thus China's String of

---

65 Garvar, J. (2002) 'The Security Dilemma in Sina-Indian Relations', India Review, 1 (4), (October, 2002), p. 38 (1-38)

54

Pearls strategy and naval presence have serious strategic implications for Indian interests.

To safeguard these Indian strategic interests and with the alarms of Chinese naval power, Indian strategists called to develop power naval forces, especially to build light aircraft carrier, submarine and surface force to dominate the Indian Ocean region. In terms of geostrategic view, Port Blair in the Andaman Islands, only 500 miles from the Strait of Malacca and the Burma Coast is the most importance strategic area for India's Eastern Command in any future conflict with China. As Eric Margolis argues, India's carrier strike force, missile-armed submarines and land-based naval aviation could make Chinese naval forces at a serious disadvantage if there were not provided effective air cover from the air bases in Burma.[66] Thus, Burma factor has become the most important factor in Sino-Indian relations and both countries have taken different approaches towards the resources-rich, but poor and isolated country.

---

66 Margolis, E. (2005) 'India rules the Waves', *Proceedings*, March 2005, p. 66

On the other hand, Chinese strategist, Ma Kan from National Defense University, recently highlighted the rise of defense expenditures in India in 2009 with the efforts to build an aircraft carrier of its own, launch of first home made submarine and goals set towards possessing three dimensional nuclear strategy capability.[67] Furthermore, a researcher of the Chinese Academy of Military Science, Hao Ding, identified the shifts that have taken place in Indian Defense Strategy in terms of military power status, strategic shift of the line 'passive defense' to 'active and aggressive defense', giving China as an important emphasis from the angle of war objectives, a shift to stabilizing Western Front and strengthening Northern Front based on land and sea warfare in the matters of strategic deployment, efforts to create long-range mobile operational strength as well as the capacity to launch cross-combat missions'[68]

67 Kan, M. (2009) 'Panoramic View of International Military Situation in 2009', *Liberation Army Daily*, 29 December 2009

68 Ding, H.(2009) 'Great changes in India's Defense Strategy- War objective shifts to giving China importance, while treating Pakistan as lightweight', *China Youth Daily*, 27 November 2009

and urged Beijing leadership to eye on Indian moves.

In fact, there are a wide range of different views and images on Sino-Indian relationship among the Chinese and Indian scholars from potential military conflicts to power rivalries. Nevertheless, both countries would not push themselves to be locked in confrontation with each other, except in extreme circumstances as the primary objectives of the security strategy of China and India are economic development and favorable security environment. Based on geopolitics, there are unavoidable competitive elements in Sino-Indian relations in terms of strategic capabilities and power struggles, however, competition may not be over exaggerated for the zero-sum games.

China and the littoral states: Burma and Pakistan as case studies

"China is building strategic relationships along the sea lanes from the Middle East to the South China Sea in a way that suggests defensive and offensive positioning to protect China's energy interests."

(Jason Blazevic)[69]

China-Pakistan Relations

Since its founding, Beijing foreign policy has given high priority to strategic relations with the countries of Asia, Africa and Latin America, which have been referred to as 'Third World'. By supporting revolutionary 'national liberalization struggles' during the 1960s, 'self-reliant development' during the 1970s and 'Asia Values' during the

69 Blazevic, J. (2009) 'Defensive Realism in the Indian Ocean: Oil, Sea Lanes and the Security Dilemma', *China Security*, 5 (3), pp. 63 (59-71)

1990s, China has principally sought to establish the durable strategic relations with the countries of Asia, especially the littoral states in the Indian Ocean.

In terms of the strategic relations with Pakistan, Sino-Pakistani relations has been referred to as 'a friendship higher than the peaks of Himalayas', as the Pakistan President[70] declared in 2009. With the establishment of diplomatic ties from 1951 to the middle of the decade, Pakistan was the third non-Communist state and first Muslim state to recognize the People's Republic of China. Despite of the cooled relationships in the late 1950s due to the vote of Pakistan with the United States to postpone a vote on seating China in the United Nations, Pakistan then signed a landmark boundary agreement with China in March 1963. It was followed by an Air Service Agreement that had the effect of ending the isolation of China through the extension of Pakistan Airlines to its territory. In return, China also became a reliable source of military hardware

---

70 Zardari, A. (2009) 'Sino-Pakistan relations higher than Himalaya",
   China Daily, August 17, 2009

during a period that was growing Western restrictions and embargoes on Pakistan.[71]

After the Soviet Invasion of Afghanistan in 1979, both China and Pakistan were in total agreement that the Soviet military presence in Afghanistan could be assumed as a threat to the security of the entire region. Thus, "support to Pakistan's security was the major feature of China's Afghanistan policy because they wanted to honour their often repeated commitments'[72], as stated by the strategic analyst, Fazal-Rehman. Chinese President Ziaul Haq also asserted that the two countries had a "perfect understanding in all fields"[73] in 1980. By that time, there had a steady development of Sino-Pakistani relations and continuous strengthening of cooperation between the two political leadership.

71 Bhatty, M, (2000) 'Pak-China relations in the 21st Century', *Regional Studies (Islamabad)*, Vol. XVIIII, No.1, p.82
72 Rehman, F. (1998) 'Pakistan's Relations with China', Strategic Studies (Islamabad Policy Research Institute)), XIX (14), pp.72
73 Pakistan Times, 20 May 1980

Later, the relations were more consolidated with the exchange of visits between the leaders of the countries. In October 1982, China-Pakistan Joint Committee of Economy, Trade and Technology was also set up for economic cooperation along with the military and diplomatic ties. The most concrete nature of the Sino-Pakistani relations can be further seen in the opening in 1982 of the Karakoram Highway that connects Kashgar in China's Xinjiang Uighur Autonomous Region with Islamabad as China's Deputy Premier Li Xiannian publicly stated that 'the highway allows China to give military aid to Pakistan'[74].(Figure-5) Explicitly, it was constructed with the purpose of fostering trade and people-to-people contact, however, implicitly, it was for the purpose of enhancing both countries' political and logistical control over their frontiers and capability to deal with external and internal security threats.

---

74 This opening speech was quoted in Haider, Z. (2005) 'Sino-Pakistan Relations and Xinjang's Uighors: Politics, Trade and Islam along the Karakoram Highway', *Asian Survey*, 45 (4), p. 522 (522-545)

Since then, Sino-Pakistani relations has been further developed into a 'all-weather' relations. When Pakistan was sanctioned by Washington in 1990, China had earned a more stronger friendship with the ruling establishment than the United States by means of the continuous 'promised' supply of weapons. Although Washington resumed its military and economic support to Islamabad after 9/11, the relations between China and Pakistan had already heightened, as retired Pakistan Army Lieutenant General, Talat Masood stated, "'Pakistan trusts the Chinese much more than others and China has remained a close friend, an ally and, above all, an important emerging global power".[75]

In terms of Defense ties, China is Pakistan's largest defense supplier and China has supported all efforts of military modernization programs in Pakistan. Throughout the 1980s and 1990s, it was China that enhanced the role of Pakistan in South-Asian Strategic Balance by supplying ballistic missile programs. In 1992, China

---

75 Quoted in Bokhari, F. (2009) 'Pakistan seeks to build on bonds with China', *Jane's Defence Weekly*, 7 December, 2009

supplied Pakistan with 34 short-range ballistic M-11 missiles[76] to strengthen military cooperation between the two countries.

In the region's changing strategic environment in the 21st Century, China and Pakistan have more collaborated in aviation and naval defense systems and forged a formidable partnership in developing high-tech defense production. In 2009, the J-10[77] sale deal that marked the depth of a strategic alliance between China and Pakistan were revealed. According to China Brief, the J-10 deal was reportedly sealed for a whopping $1.4 billion, which accounts for 70 percent of Chinese average arms sales of $2 billion a year.[78] They have also set out for the joint production of JF-17 combat aircraft that both countries consider a substitute for U.S. F-16s since 2003. China

---

76 Faruqui, "*The Complex Dynamics of Pakistan's Relationship with China*," Islamabad Policy Research Institute (Summer 2001), at http://www.ipripak.org/journal/summer2001/thecomplex.shtml (accessed on 12/1/2010)

77 The J-10 is the China's third generation fighter aircraft roughly equivalent in capabilities to the U.S. F-16C flown by several air forces around the world.

78 China Brief, July 9, 2009

has also helped Pakistan Navy to build the F-22P frigates with a $250 million non-commercial loan since 2004[79]. Traditionally, the military doctrine of Pakistan more focused on the power of ground forces than naval and air power. However, the new developments has shifter from the traditional focus to the interests of naval defense. Tarique Niazi, asserted that the shift of the military doctrine of Pakistan is dependent on the growing stake of China in the Indian Ocean region.[80]

In fact, in the eyes of Chinese strategists, the enduring relations with Pakistan strongly support its interests in countering Indian power as well as diverting strategic attention of Indian military forces away from China. In her testimony before the U.S.-China Economic and Security Review Commission on May 20, 2009, Lisa Curtis clearly stated the view of Chinese officials in terms of 'a certain degree of India-Pakistan tension as advancing their own strategic interests as

79 The News International, September 16, 2004
80 Niazi, T. (2009) 'J-10: The New Cornerstone of Sino-Pakistani Defense Cooperation', China Brief, December 16, 2009

such friction bogs India down in South Asia and interferes with New Delhi's ability to assert its global ambitions and compete with China at the international level' by demonstrating the role of Beijing as 'it favors bilateral Indo-Pakistani negotiations to resolve their differences and has played a helpful role in preventing the outbreak of full-scale war between the two countries,especially during the 1999 Indo-Pakistani border conflict in the heights of Kargil.[81]

John Garver also states that he China-Pakistan partnership serves both Chinese and Pakistani interests by presenting India with a potential two-front theater in the event of war with either country. [82] However, in the minds of Beijing strategists in the 21st century, the logic of 'defense perimeter of the Pacific', i.e., the United States and

---

81 Curtis, L. (2009) *China's Military and Security Relationship with Pakistan*', Testimony before US-China Economic and Security Review Commission, May 20, 2009, http://www.heritage.org/RESEARCH/ASIAANDTHEPACIFIC/tst05 2609a.cfm#_ftn3 (12/1/2010)

82 Garver (2001) *Protracted Contest: Sino-Indian Rivalry in the Twentieth Century*, Seattle, University of Washington Press, p. 188.

its allies can "encircle" China,[83] "squeez[e] China's strategic space,"[84] or "blockade the Asian mainland (China in particular)"[85] from island strongholds where powerful naval expeditionary forces are based, seems to be more occupied rather than the military confrontation with India. Thus, China seek to secure beacheads in the Indian Ocean basin by cultivating closer relationships with the littoral states and Pakistan seems to be one of the most important strategic zones.

Although, the term of the 'String of Pearls' strategy has derived from the US observers and not codified in Chinese strategic doctrine, the construction of port facilities in Gwadar in Western Pakistan, could be seen as one of the pearls that can be drawn from the Chinese patterns of behavior in the Indian Ocean. Gwadar was the status of a

83 Editorial, 'US-Indian Alliance Against China', *Ming Pao*, August 17, 2005
84 Tong, Q. (2002) '2002: Focus on Guam', *Kuang Chiao Ching*, October 16, 2002
85 Wang, J.; Feng, N, and Liping, Z. (2004) 'Impact of US Global Strategic Adjustment on China', Zhongguo Shabui Kexueyuan Yuanbao, January 7, 2004

third Deep Sea Port of Pakistan which has a special significance with reference to trade links with Central Asian Countries, Persian Gulf, East Africa, United Arab Emirates and North Western India. Although Pakistan military strategists have planned to develop Gwardar into a naval place since the years after Indo-Pakistan War of 1971, the real Gwadar project only came up with the Sino-Pakistan agreement in March, 2002, with a vision to become a regional hub serving incoming and outgoing commercial traffic of the Middle Eastern and Gulf countries, the Xinjiang province of China, Iran in the west and Sri Lanka and Bangladesh in the south and east. Moreover, it is strategically located near the Strait of Hormus, thus, the new port would provide both economic and military opportunities for Beijing.

In his testimony before the US-China Economic and Security Review Commission in 2007, Professor James Holmes from U.S. Army War College, identified the strategic interests of China in Gwadar Port (Figure- 5) In terms of energy security and military opportunity. He clearly points out tha 'Gwadar could act as a strategic hedge, giving

Beijing a workaround should the United States blockade the Malacca Strait during a Taiwan contingency or some other Sino-U.S Clash as Persian Gulf oil could be offloaded at the port and transported (or pumped, should plans for a pipeline bear fruit) overland to China', whereas, in terms of military standpoint, 'Gwadar offers a useful installation for monitoring commercial and military traffic passing through the critical chokepoint at Hormuz and over the longer term, should China develop a navy robust enough to project credible power into the Indian Ocean, then the port promises to allow Beijing to directly shape events in the Persian Gulf.'[86]

86 Holmes, J. (2007) 'China's Energy Consumption and Opportunities for US-China Cooperation to address the effects of China's energy use', Testimony before the U.S- China Economic and Strategic Review Commision, June 14, 2007. http://www.uscc.gov/hearings/2007hearings/transcripts/june_14_1 5/holmes_prepared_remarks.pdf (14/1/2009)

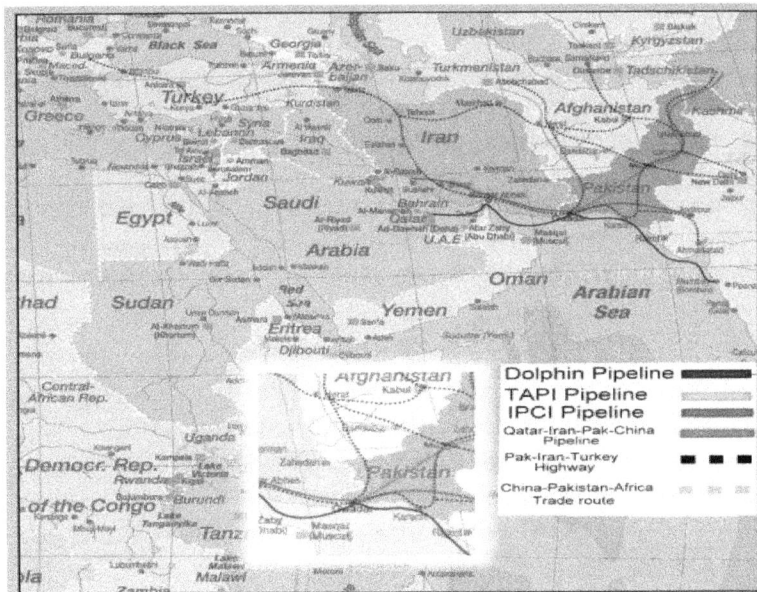

Figure 5- Strategic significance of Gwadar

Furthermore, the construction of the port has made the dreams of Pakistan's political leadership into reality. It was clearly reflected in the words of Masood Khan, Pakistan Foreign Ministry Spokesman in 2004, as 'The Gwadar port is a symbol of Pak-China cooperation and is part of our joint efforts to build modern infrastructure projects in Pakistan. Once built, the port will act as a strategic hub for

69

commercial activity for the entire region'.[87] However, while China and Pakistan believe that the port would bring significant economic gains and military opportunities, on the other hand, India and Iran may view it as a potential threat to their security and economic interests as well as the United States and Japan view it as the signal of the rising power of China.

Sino-Myanmar Relations (China-Burma Relations)

Sino-Myanmar Relations has been regarded as a 'comprehensive, stable and lasting relations'.[88] Since ancient times, the peoples of the two countries have lived in harmony with a special traditional 'Paukphaw' (meaning brothers) friendly relationship. When PRC was founded in 1949, Burma (Myanmar)[89] was the first country which

---

87 "Beijing Lauds Best Medical Care to Injured Chinese," The News (Pakistan), 6 May 2004.

88 China Daily, June 16, 2009

89 The name of the country, Myanmar, predates the name Burma, and was revived by the military regime in 1989. It is now recognized by the United Nations, though the United States, Britain and some other countries continue to employ the name

recognized PRC and forged formal diplomatic relations in June, 1950. In 1953, Premier Zhou Enlai proposed the "Five Principles for Peaceful Coexistence"[90] to the Indian diplomats and at the end of June 1954, Premier Zhou visited India and Myanmar to have some talks with prime ministers of the two countries separately. A Sino-Burmese Joint Declaration of the 29th June, 1954, reiterated that the five principles for peaceful coexistence serve as guiding principles for bilateral relations. For several years, these bilateral relations have witnessed a stable development except for for the aforementioned anti-Chinese riots which occurred in the late 1960s, as both sides adhere to good-neighborhood and pursue a path of co-

---

Burma as a way of protesting against the present military government (that carried out the name change). The European Union has chosen to compromise and refers to Myanmar/Burma. In this study, the name Myanmar may from time to time be used interchangeably with Burma, depending on the context.

90 These principles include: (1) mutual respect for each other's sovereignty and territorial integrity; (2) non-aggression; (3) non-interference in each other's internal affairs; (4) equality and mutual benefit; and (5) peaceful coexistence. Later the principles were adopted by the Non-Aligned Movement as the basis for international relations.

operation in both international and regional affairs.

By analyzing the ups and downs of Sino-Myanmar relations, Lixin Geng divided the relations from 1950 to the present into four phases such as 'ambivalent peaceful coexistence, 1949-1961; temporary setbacks, 1962-1970; improved relations, 1971-1988; and closer ties, 1989-present.'[91] The first phase of modern China-Burma relations involves a high degree of political engagement with the Sino-Burmese Joint Declaration in 1954. However, the border dispute was culminated in 1956, when the People's Liberation Army invaded northern Burma and later settled in 1960 with the Sino-Burmese Boundary Treaty, which was hailed by the two governments as a model of how Asian nations should settle the historical border-disputes.[92] Thereafter, the Sino-Burmese relations was deteriorated again in the late 1960s with the emergence of anti-Chinese riots in

---

91 Gang, L. (2006) 'Sino-Myanmar relations: Analysis and Prospects', 7 (2) (December, 2006), p. 2 (1-15)

92 Whittan, D. (1961) 'The Sino-Burmese Boundary Treaty', *Pacific Affairs*, 34 (2) ,(Summer, 1961), pp. 174 (174-183)

Burma.

In May 1967, Chinese Embassy personnel distributed Maoist propaganda and 'encouraged Chinese students to form groups patterned after the Red Guard'[93], and urged them to defy the government on wearing of political insignia, i.e. the Mao Badges. However, these activities led to bloody clashes between Burmese and Chinese and, as a result, anti-Chinese riots were spreading throughout the Capital of Burma, bringing hundreds of Chinese owned shops and homes as well as the Chinese embassy under attack.[94] The relations reached to a low point and in March, 1969, Burma gave notice to China that 'The friendship and mutual non-aggression Treaty would be terminated after it is over on May 14, 1970'. Therefore, these years were referred to as a period of 'temporary setbacks' in Sino-Burmese relations.

---

93 Holmes, R. (1972) 'China-Burma Relations since the Rift', *Asian Survey*, 12 (8), (August, 1972), pp. 689 (686-700)

94 Trager, F. (1968) 'Sino-Burmese Relations: The End of the Pauk-Phaw Era', *Orbis*, XI: 4 (Winter, 1968), pp. 1039-1045

However, the relations began to improve in the early 1970s with bilateral trade agreements and high-level visits between the state leaders of Beijing and Rangoon. In the late 1970s, with the reinstatement of Deng Xiaoping and his plans to modernize China, the improving relationships with South-east Asian countries became at the onset of China's economic reform.[95] Then, Deng visited Burma in 1978 as the first visit to the foreign country by the highest Chinese leadership in the wake of the Culture Revolution. Since then, the Kuming- Rangoon route became the focal point of state visits and the provincial government of Yunnan played a key role in facilitating bilateral relations between China and Burma.

During the 1990s, the two countries forged a closer relationship in

---

95 Guo, X. (2007) 'Towards Resolution: China in the Myanmar issue', *Silk Road Paper*, Central Asia- Cacasus Institute and the Silk Road Studies Program, Sweden, p. 47

http://www.isdp.eu/files/publications/ap/07/xg07towardsresolution.pdf (accessed on 15/1/2010)

response to the international isolation following the crackdowns of the protestors in August, 1988 in Burma and in June, 1989 in China. In terms of diplomatic isolation and economic collapse, Burma turned to China for economic assistance and military aids. As Lin argued, China helped Myanmar to strengthen its consolidated power through three means such as 'provision of advanced weapons, assistance in building military installations and facilitating the peace dialogue between the military government and the anti-government armed groups through its own influence.'[96] China is the major arms supplier for the military junta of Burma. A year after the crackdown on the protests, the first military delegation arrived in Beijing to negotiate for the deal of the supply of arms.[97] China also agreed to provide training for Burmese military officers from navy and air force.

Moreover, China has given a massive offers of free loans and

---

96 Lin, X. (1999) 'Myanmar's Policy towards China after the Cold War', Southeast Asian Studies, No.4, pp.31
97 Seekins, D. M. (1997) 'Burma-China Relations: Playing with Fire', Asian Survey, 3 (6), p.534

granted credits to the military junta for Myanmar's arms purchases as well as economic aids and direct investments for the construction of the country's infrastructure. Significantly, China supported the construction of strategic roads along the Irrawaddy Trade route that links between the Bay of Bengal and Yunnan province. In June 1999, the leaders of both sides further reached the consensus on working towards a sustainable, stable and co-operative relationship oriented towards the 21st century[98]. Since then, both China and Myanmar have maintained this consensus through military and intelligence co-operation, diplomatic ties and economic and trade links.

In terms of economic links, the bilateral trade between Myanmar and China has increased with the establishment of Myanmar-China Economic Enhancement Committee. Under the economic and technical cooperation between the two countries, Chinese companies have initiated a large number of projects in Myanmar,

---

98 Shee, P. K. (2002) 'The Political Economy of China-Myanmar Relations: Strategic and Economic Dimensions, Ritsumeikan Annual Review of International Studies, Vol. 1, pp. 40 (33-53)

covering hydro-power plants, commercial network projects, cement and paper plants, agricultural machinery factories, bridge projects and processing of forest and marine products. While strengthening economic and technical cooperation, the two leadership established a stronger and closer diplomatic ties through frequent exchanges of high-level visits. In the anticipation of the 60th anniversary of Sino-Myanmar diplomatic ties in June, 2010, Chinese Ambassador Ye asserted that China would push deeply the continuous development of friendly and mutually-beneficial cooperation of the two countries in every sector.[99]

In terms of military co-operation, for several years, China has supplied a bulk of military equipments including tanks, armoured personnel carriers, military aircraft and artillery pieces such as howitzers, anti-tank guns and anti-aircraft guns, etc. In 1998, China reported to the United Nations that it had delivered US$5.9 million worth of military equipment to Myanmar under a trade category

99 China Daily, September 29, 2009

entitled "tanks and other armoured fighting vehicles", and US$3.4 million of "military weapons'.[100] In 2002, China also reported to the UN that it delivered 3,200 firearms to Myanmar, and in 2004, China reported the deliveries of US$1,155,067 of parts and accessories for weapons.[101] Furthermore, since 1998, at least 14 Karakorum K-8 light attack aircraft, co-developed by China and Pakistan, have been reportedly transferred to Myanmar. [102] In 2009, the Chief of the General Staff of PLA, also firmly remarked that "China is willing to further maintain and strengthen friendly military cooperation with Myanmar." [103]

Among the various forms of assistance and military ties, the most significant events involved China's assistance in establishing naval

100 UN Comtrade 1998 Classification SITC Rev 3 Codes 89111 and 89112.
101. UN Comtrade 2002 Classification SITC Rev 3 Code 89131 and 1997, 1999, 2001 and 2004 Code 89199
102. 'Myanmar's military links with Pakistan", Jane's Intelligence Review 1 June 2000
103. China Daily, April 29, 2009

bases on Hianggyi Island in the Irrawaddy River Delta and in the Great Coco Island in the Indian Ocean, approximately 30 nautical miles from India's Andaman Islands. Some further argued that China has also built naval facilities, radars and signal-intelligence (SIGINT) posts all along the Myanmar coast and in the Coco Islands[104] and in June, 2008, a Chinese naval team visited Coco Island upgrade its military facilities.[105] However, both Chinese and Myanmar authorities have repeatedly denied that there were any Chinese bases on Great Coco Islands or elsewhere. [106] Whether it is a reality or myth, these claims must have exaggerated from the geo-strategic reality of Burma, Beijing's closer relations with the military junta and the strategic interests of China in the Indian Ocean.

104.'Chinese electronic fishing in the Andamans', Asian Defense Journal, December, 1994; 'India says China has surveillance base in Myanmar', Reuters, 3 May 1998; Selth, A.(2007) 'Chinese Military Bases in Burma: The Explosion of a Myth', Regional Outlook No.10. Griffith Asia Institute, Brisbane, etc.
105. Bagchi, I., 'China eyeing base', Times of India, August 9, 2008
106. See, for example, 'Myanmar denies China using its island as a base', Reuters, 5 May 1998

As a littoral state in the Indian Ocean, Myanmar's strategic value has been increasing, especially in terms of energy security, strategic land bridge between South and Southeast Asia and its 1930 km long coastline dominating the eastern arch of the Bay of Bengal, leaning onto the Malacca Strait. As Hariharan, a retired military intelligence analyst who specializes in South Asia, points out, Myanmar provides China the shortest land and sea access to South Asia, just as it provides convenient external land and sea communication options to India's landlocked northeastern states. [107]

By recognizing these strategic values, Beijing's policy towards Myanmar since 1990s have based on political and security considerations, economic considerations and energy security. As PLA Navy could reach to the Indian Ocean via Myanmar-controlled islands which are near to Indian-controlled islands have put the

107. Hariharan, R. (2007) 'India-China-Myanmar Relations', Paper presented to 'An Interaction on Emerging India-China-Myanmar Relations', jointly organized by the Chenna Centre for China Studies and Stella Maris College, India on 19, July, 2007

strategic imperative of Myanmar in the eyes of Chinese strategists. Moreover, the PLAN would be able to shorten the distance by 3000 km to reach to the Bay of Bengal, without passing through the Malacca Strait. In terms of economic considerations, China is a major player in several fields such as hydro-power projects[108], Banking and Finance. Yunnan Province also seeks 'a direct access route through Myanmar to sea ports from which it can export products to South Asia, the Middle East and Europe' that would reduce transport costs and time, and avoid the Malacca Strait in the event of a conflict in the South China Sea.

In terms of energy resources, Chinese oil corporations have invested in Myanmar's oil and gas fields since 2004 and PetroChina have built a gas pipeline from the A-1 block in the Shwe field off the coast of Rahine State to Yunnan Province. In the early 2009, China began the construction of oil and gas pipelines from the Kyaukpyu port on the Bay of Bengal in proximity to the Yunnan Province, a US $2.5 billion

108. 'Chinese consortium, Myanmar sign largest hydropower project contracts', People's daily, 15th July 2005

project that was inked pipeline project in November 2008. Moreover, Strategic analysts argue that Kyaukphyu port was also a part of the 'String of Pearls' strategy in geopolitics, involving the extension of its influence in both the Pacific and India oceans, while reducing China's dependence on the Straits of Malacca. Whether it is a pearl or not, it is obvious that Kyaukphyu gas pipeline would provide an alternative route for China to get access to the Indian Ocean via Myanmar and is of strategic importance for Chinese interests in the 21st century.

Looking to the Future

Sea Power

Sir Walter Ralegh once mentioned that 'Whosoever commands the sea commands the trade; whoever commands the trade of the world commands the riches of the world, and consequently the world itself'[109]. These sayings clearly reflect the Current Security Environment that the focus of global strategic concerns has shifted to the Indian Ocean region. For China, its national goals have been shifting from the need of survival to the state of stable economic development. To fulfill these goals, it not only requires to fully integrate with the global market, but also, access to energy resources. Thus, China has to plot its strategy on energy security and protect its vulnerabilities at any costs.

In the eyes of Chinese strategists, maritime transportation in the Indian Ocean is a key factor for the overwhelming success of the

---

109.cited in Tangredi, p. 117

flow of goods and commodities for the economy, therefore a powerful navy able to effectively control the sea passages and protect the vital SLOCs is required to be built. Hence, the paramount concerns animating Chinese strategic interests in the Indian Ocean have prompted China to attempt to pursue Sea Power, that could be measured by Mahanian indices of commerce, bases and ships. However, its strive for Sea Power has been seen by the great powers as a future strategic challenge that would pose to them in the long term. Will the future role of China in the Indian Ocean be stable and defensive or destructive and offensive?

Some analysts answered this question based on the aspects of strategic culture of China that 'China may undertake an offensive foreign policy at the point of time when Chinese leaders think the international balance of power is in their favor.'[110] In contrast, some

---

110. Mattoo, A. (1999) "Shadow of the Dragon: Indo-US Relations and China" in Gary K. Bertsch, Seema Gahlaut and Anupam Srivastava, eds., *Engaging India: US Strategic Relations with the World's Largest Democracy*, New York: Routledge, pp.217-8.

analysts argue that the 'rising China' had emerged from the the dilemmas and insecurities posed by its dependence on the public goods posed by the US Navy.[111] Some also assume that China will encounter an equally sea-power-minded India that enjoys marked geostrategic advantages.[112] In fact, the future role of China in the Indian Ocean in terms of 'stable rising power' or 'destructive rising power' would be dependent on the strategic relations among US-China-India Strategic Triangle and the possible emergence of Asian security architecture.

US-China-India Strategic Triangle

In recent years, the United States has actively participated in several multilateral forums such as the ASEAN Regional Forum (ARF), the Six-Party Talks, the Asia-Pacific Economic Cooperation (APEC) and engaged with the various security issues of the Asia-Pacific region.

Besides these multilateral approaches, the United States and Japan have established the trilateral security cooperation with India. Since 2005, US policy makers perceive India as the main geopolitical actor in Asia and signed a Defense Framework with India and issue a joint declaration of 'global partnership'. On the other hand, the United States also attempted to augment its political, economic and military relationships with China under the banner of 'transformational diplomacy' since 2006.

Meanwhile, China-India joint communique has been signed by the political leadership with the establishment of peace and prosperity-oriented strategic co-operative partnership. In the context of Asia-Pacific region, the strategic relationships between these three countries will dominate the future events of Indian Ocean as well as the region as a whole. If these countries push out their differences by seeking out common interests in the Indian Ocean and establish a harmonious relationship based on mutual understanding, there would be, to the large extent, peace and stability in the region.

However, if the leaders of the three countries give first priorities on arms racing, maritime rivalries, regional dominance, ideological conflicts and miscalculations of the intent and capabilities of potential adversaries towards each other, there would be military confrontations, proxy wars and instability in the region. Thus, their interactions and managing strategic relations with the triangle and other littoral states would determine whether Indian Ocean would become at the center of 21st century struggles or not, as predicted by Robert Kaplan. To have a harmonious strategic relation for peace and stability in the region, the establishment of Organization for Security and Cooperation in Asia (OSCA), led by US-China-India Strategic Triangle, is recommended.

Comprehensive Approach to Security

For many years, the nature of Asian Security Environment has been characterized by unwarranted fears, armed struggles and revolutions, ideological conflicts, wars and military rivalries, authoritarianism and military coups, militant ethnic identities, political disasters, security deficits, major/minor conflicts and absences of common desire for collective security. Thus a comprehensive approach to security should be encouraged among the Asian leaders under the leadership of the global power, the United States and the regional powers, China and India. Recent emerging trends in the security architecture in Asia, i.e. bilateral and multilateral ties among United States, Japan, Australia and India may contribute to Asian-Pacific regional security as a whole, these trends could be perceived by China as an attempt to contain China. Likewise, with the mis-interpretations and miscalculations of Chinese strategic ambitions and capabilities, unwarranted fears and 'China Threat' syndromes or misuses of China's sphere of influence could be spread among the Asian nations. To overcome these possible Cold War mentalities, the multilateral initiative, like, OSCE[113] in Europe should be adopted in Asia.

---

113. The OSCE is the world's largest regional security organization whose 56 participating States span the geographical area from Vancouver to Vladivostok.

The new security architecture in the form of Organization for Security and Co-operation in Asia could pursue the comprehensive security approach encompassing politico-military dimension, economic and environmental dimension and human dimension, as similar to the three baskets formulated in the Helsinki Final Act 1975[114]. As the politico-military dimension could enhance military security by promoting greater openness, transparency and cooperation, it may reduce the potential armed conflicts arising from miscalculations of capabilities and intent of potential adversaries, along with the Confidence and Security Building measures (CSBMs). Through these measures and comprehensive approach to security, cooperation among the fields of politics, economics, military and

---

114. The Final Act of the Conference on Security and Cooperation in Europe, known as the Helsinki Final Act, Helsinki Accords or Helsinki Declaration, was the final act of the Conference on Security and Co-operation in Europe held in Helsinki, Finland during July and August of 1975. Thirty-five states, including the USA, Canada, and all European states except Albania and Andorra, signed the declaration in an attempt to improve relations between the two blocs

human affairs could be strengthened. There is no doubt that stability in the Indian Ocean is essential in the 21st century and the potential global struggles could only be prevented by boosting the efforts to involve in multilateral security arrangements, rather than attempting to counter as a threat.

Bibliography

Asian Defense Journal, December, 1994

Bagchi, I., 'China eyeing base', Times of India, August 9, 2008

Bhatty, M, (2000) 'Pak-China relations in the 21st Century', *Regional Studies (Islamabad)*, Vol. XVIIII, No.1

Blazevic, J. (2009) 'Defensive Realism in the Indian Ocean: Oil, Sea Lanes and the Security Dilemma', *China Security*, 5 (3), pp. 63 (59-71)

Bodeen, C. (2008) Indian Ocean is Chinese Lake: 'String of Pearls' threaten India, AP News, 29/8/2008

Bokhari, F. (2009) 'Pakistan seeks to build on bonds with China', *Jane's Defence Weekly*, 7 December, 2009

Braun, D. (1983) *The Indian Ocean: Region of Conflict or 'Peace Zone*, St. Martin's Press, New York

Chellaney, B. (2008) 'Dragon in India's backyard', *Asia Age*, December 31, 2008

Cheng, J. & Wankun (2004) 'Patterns and Dynamics of China's

International Strategic Behaviour', in Zhao, S. (ed.) *Chinese Foreign Policy: Pragmatism and Strategic Behaviour*, East Gate, New York

China Brief, July 9, 2009

China Daily, May 19, 1998

China Youth Daily, June 15, 2004

China Daily, 12 June, 2005

China Daily, July 2, 2008

China Daily, June 16, 2009

China Youth Daily, April, 2009

China Daily, 1st April, 2009

China Daily, September 29, 2009

China News Digest-Global, December 12, 1998

Clinton, W. (2004) *My Life*, Knopf

Commentator, 'New Trends in the Current International Strategic Situation', *International Strategic Studies (Beijing)*, No.1 (January,

1997)

Cohen, S. B. (1973) *Geography and politics in a world divided*, Oxford University Press, Oxford

Curtis, L. (2009) '*China's Military and Security Relationship with Pakistan*', Testimony before US-China Economic and Security Review Commission, May 20, 2009, http://www.heritage.org/RESEARCH/ASIAANDTHEPACIFIC/tst0526 09a.cfm#_ftn3 (12/1/2010)

Davidovv, . F. and Kremenyukv, . A. (1973) 'Strategiya SSHAV. Zone Indiyskovo Okeana', U.S.A.: Econ. Pol. Ideol. 5: 6-17 (Moscow)

Devonshire-Ellis, C. (2009) China's String of Pearls Strategy, China Briefing online, http://www.china-briefing.com/news/2009/03/18/china%E2%80%99s-string-of-pearls-strategy.html (accessed on 23/12/2009)

'Rapid Naval Growth in Asia', *Defense Review Asia Magazine*, December, 2009

Ding, H.(2009) 'Great changes in India's Defense Strategy- War objective shifts to giving China importance, while treating Pakistan as lightweight', *China Youth Daily*, 27 November 2009

DNA Inida, May 11, 2009

Editorial, 'US-Indian Alliance Against China', Ming Pao, August 17, 2005

Faruqui, "*The Complex Dynamics of Pakistan's Relationship with China*," Islamabad Policy Research Institute (Summer 2001), at http://www.ipripak.org/journal/summer2001/thecomplex.shtml (accessed on 12/1/2010)

Fenggang, Z. (2006) "The Impact of the Maritime Strategies of Asia-Pacific Nations," Dangdai Yatai , 5

Gang, L. (2006) 'Sino-Myanmar relations: Analysis and Prospects', 7 (2) (December, 2006), p. 1-15

Garrett, B. & Glaser, B. (1997) 'Chinese Apprehensions about Revitalization of the U.S.-Japan alliance', *Asian Survey*, 37 (4), p. 385-386

Garrison, J. (2005) *Making China Policy: From Nixon to G.W. Bush*, Lynne Rienner, London

Garvar, J. (2002) 'The Security Dilemma in Sina-Indian Relations', *India Review*, 1 (4), (October, 2002), pp.1-38

Garver (2001) *Protracted Contest: Sino-Indian Rivalry in the Twentieth Century*, Seattle, University of Washington Press

Godwin, P. (1998) 'Force and Diplomacy: China Prepares for the Twenty-First Century', in Kim, S.(ed) *China and the World: Chinese Foreign Policy faces the new Millennium,* 4th edition, Westview Press, Oxford

Guo, X. (2007) 'Towards Resolution: China in the Myanmar issue', *Silk Road Paper,* Central Asia- Cacasus Institute and the Silk Road Studies Program, Sweden, p. 47
http://www.isdp.eu/files/publications/ap/07/xg07towardsresolution.pdf (accessed on 15/1/2010)

Haider, Z. (2005) 'Sino-Pakistan Relations and Xinjang's Uighors: Politics, Trade and Islam along the Karakoram Highway', *Asian Survey,* 45 (4), pp. 522-545

Han, H. (1998) 'Sino-Indian relations and nuclear arms control', in Arett, E. (ed.) *Nuclear Weapons and arms control in South Asia after the test ban,* SIPRI Research Report No.14, New York, Oxford University Press

Hariharan, R. (2007) 'India-China-Myanmar Relations', Paper presented to 'An Interaction on Emerging India-China-Myanmar Relations', jointly organized by the Chenna Centre for China Studies and Stella Maris College, India on 19, July, 2007

Holmes, J. (2007) 'China's Energy Consumption and Opportunities for US-China Cooperation to address the effects of China's energy use', Testimony before the U.S- China Economic and Strategic Review Commision, June 14, 2007. http://www.uscc.gov/hearings/2007hearings/transcripts/june_14_15/holmes_prepared_remarks.pdf (14/1/2009)

Holmes, R. (1972) 'China-Burma Relations since the Rift', *Asian Survey*, 12 (8), (August, 1972), pp. 686-700

Ji, Y. (2007) 'Dealing with the Malacca Dilemma: China's Effort to protect Energy's Supply', *Strategic Analysis,* 31(3), (May, 2007), pp. 523-542

'Myanmar's military links with Pakistan", *Jane's Intelligence Review,* 1 June 2000

Kan, M. (2009) 'Panoramic View of International Military Situation in 2009', *Liberation Army Daily*, 29 December 2009

Kaplan, R. (2009) 'Center Stage for the 21st Century: Power Plays in the Indian Ocean', *Foreign Affairs*, (March / April, 2009) http://www.realclearpolitics.com/articles/2009/03/rivalry_in_the_indian_ocean.html (accessed 2/11/2009)

Kim, S. (1991) 'Mainland China and a New World Order', in *Issues and Studie* 27, No.11 (November, 1991)

Klien, D. (1998) 'Japan and Europe in Chinese Foreign Relations', in Kim, S.(ed) *China and the World: Chinese Foreign Policy faces the New Millennium*, 4th edition, Westview Press, Oxford, p.142

Lamb, A. (1964) The China-India Border: The origins of the Disputed Boundaries, London, Oxford University Press

Levine, S. (1998)'Sini-American Relations' in Kim, S.(ed) China and the World: Chinese Foreign Policy faces the new Millennium, 4th edition, Westview Press, Oxford

Li, N. (2009) 'The Evolution of China's Naval Strategy and Capabilities: From 'Near Coast' and 'Near Seas' to 'Far seas', *Asian Security*, 5 (2), (May 2009), pp.144-169

Lin, X. (1999) 'Myanmar's Policy towards China after the Cold War', Southeast Asian Studies, No.4

Malik, M. (1999) "India-China relations in the 21st Century: The Continuing Rivalry", Brahma Chellaney edited, *Securing India's Future in the New Millennium*, Orient Longman

Margolis, E. (2005) 'India rules the Waves', *Proceedings*, March 2005

Matsuda, Y. & Saito, M. (2008) 'China: Hu Jintao Sets a Fres Course Amidst Diverse Challenges', in Ogawa, S. (eds.) *East Asian Strategic Review: 2008,* The National Institute for Defense Studies,

Japan, The Japan Times

Mattoo, A. (1999) "Shadow of the Dragon: Indo-US Relations and China" in Gary K. Bertsch, Seema Gahlaut and Anupam Srivastava, eds., *Engaging India: US Strategic Relations with the World's Largest Democracy*, New York, Routledge

Mugombaa., T. (1976) 'NATO, the SouthernO ceans and SouthernA frica', *A fr. Rev.* 6: 15-33

Niazi, T. (2009) 'J-10: The New Cornerstone of Sino-Pakistani Defense Cooperation', China Brief, December 16, 2009

Noorani, A. (1970) 'India's Forward Policy', *The China Quarterly*, No.43 (July-September 1970), p. 136-141

Office of the Secretary of Defense (2009) *Military Power of the People's Republic of China 2009*, A report to the Congress, U.S. Department of Defense, http://www.defense.gov/pubs/pdfs/China_Military_Power_Report_20 09.pdf (accessed on 12/12/2009)

Oriental Morning Post, 24th March, 2009

Pakistan Times, 20 May 1980

Peking Review, June 27, 1969

People's daily, December 1, 1992

People's daily, April 16, 1999

'Chinese consortium, Myanmar sign largest hydropower project
    contracts', People's daily, 15th July 2005

Pherson, C. (2006) *String of Pearls: Meeting the Challenges of
China's Rising Power across the Asian Littoral*, Strategic Studies
Institute, Carlisle

Qiche, Q. (1992) 'Adhering to Independent Foreign Policy', in *Beijing
Review* 34, N. 52, (Decmber, 1991- January, 1992), p.7-10

Rehman, F. (1998) 'Pakistan's Relations with China', Strategic
Studies (Islamabad Policy Research Institute)), XIX (14)

Romberg, A. (2009) "U.S. Strategic Interests in Northeast Asia: 2009
    and Beyond",
    http://www.stimson.org/eastasia/pdf/USInterests2009.pdf
    (accessed on 26/12/2009)

Ross, R. (1995) 'Negotiationg Coperation: the United States and
    China (1969-89), Stanford University Press.

'Myanmar denies China using its island as a base', *Reuters*, 5 May

1998

SCC Joint Statement(May 1, 2007) *Alliance Transformation:*
Advancing United States-Japan Security and Defense Cooperation,
http://www.mod.go.jp/e/d_policy/dp16.html (accessed on 1/1/2010)

Seekins, D. M. (1997) 'Burma-China Relations: Playing with Fire',
Asian Survey, 3 (6)

Selth, A.(2007) 'Chinese Military Bases in Burma: The Explosion of a
Myth', *Regional Outlook No.10*. Griffith Asia Institute, Brisbane

Shambaugh, D. (2005) 'The New Strategic Triangle: U.S. And
European Reactions to China's Rise, *The Washington Quarterly*, 28
(3), pp. 7-25

Shee, P. K. (2002) 'The Political Economy of China-Myanmar
Relations: Strategic and Economic Dimensions, Ritsumeikan Annual
Review of International Studies, Vol. 1, pp.33-53

Shuguang, X. & Xinjiegou, S. (1992) *The New Structure of the World*,
Chendu, Sichuan Renmin Chuban She

Spinetta, L. (2006) 'THE MALACCA DILEMMA"- Countering China's
String of Pearls with Land-based Air Power', Master's Thesis
submitted to Air University, Alabama

Storey, I. (2006) 'China's 'Malacca Dilemma', *China Brief,* 6 (8), James Stones Foundation, http://www.jamestown.org/programs/chinabrief/single/?tx_ttnews %5Btt_news%5D=31575&tx_ttnews%5BbackPid %5D=196&no_cache=1 (accessed on 13/12/2009)

Sundarji, K. (1995) *'Weapons of Mass Destruction: New Perspectives on Counterproliferation,* Institute for National Strategic Studies

Sutter,R. (2002) 'China and Japan: Troubled ahead?', *The Washington Quarterly,* 25 (4), (Autumn 2002), p.p. 37-49

Tangredi, S. (2002) 'Sea Power: Theory and Practice', in Baylis, J. al (eds) *Strategy in the contemporary World: An Introduction to Strategic Studies,* Oxford University Press, Oxford

The News International, September 16, 2004

"Beijing Lauds Best Medical Care to Injured Chinese," The News (Pakistan), 6 May 2004

Tong, Q. (2002) '2002: Focus on Guam', *Kuang Chiao Ching,* October 16, 2002

Trager, F. (1968) 'Sino-Burmese Relations: The End of the Pauk-Phaw Era', *Orbis,* XI: 4 (Winter, 1968), pp. 1039-1045

UN Comtrade 1998 Classification SITC Rev 3 Codes 89111 and 89112.

UN Comtrade 2002 Classification SITC Rev 3 Code 89131 and 1997, 1999, 2001 and 2004 Code 89199

Wang, J.; Feng, N, and Liping, Z. (2004) 'Impact of US Global Strategic Adjustment on China', *Zhongguo Shabui Kexueyuan Yuanbao*, January 7, 2004

Wenhuai, Y. (2007) 'Build a powerful Navy, Safeguard China's Maritime Strategic Interests', *Guofang 7*

Whittan, D. (1961) 'The Sino-Burmese Boundary Treaty', Pacific Affairs, 34 (2) ,(Summer, 1961), pp. 174-183

Xuetong, Y. (1998) 'The rise of China: An Evaluation of the International Environment', *Tianjin Renmin Chuban She,* p. 234-236

Yomiuri Shimbun, March 17, 1997

Zardari, A. (2009) 'Sino-Pakistan relations higher than Himalaya", *China Daily*, August 17, 2009

Zhang Y., "The Malacca Strait and World Oil Security," *Huanqiu Shibao*, Dec. 2003, in. Guo Ling, "Experts Suggest Need to Build a 'Panamal Canal' in Asia," *Wen Wei Po*, Jan. 14, 2004.

Zhao, S. (2004) 'Beijing's Perception of the International System and Foreign Policy Adjustment after the Tiananmen Incident', in Zhao, S. (ed.) *Chinese Foreign Policy: Pragmatism and Strategic Behaviour*, East Gate, New York